AF255592

Grandpa's Garden

Published by Write 'em Cowgirl Publishing
To contact the author, write to the publisher at:
trigar@mlode.com

Grandpa's Garden
by Tricia Gardella
Illustrated by Karen Donnelly

Category:
JUVENILE FICTION / Family

Paperback ISBN: 978-1-959412-267
Hardback ISBN: 978-1-959412-274
Library of Congress Control Number: available upon request

Synopsis:
Grandpa's garden is full of beautiful and healthy treats.

Edited and designed by
Emerald Books
emerald-books.com

Grandpa's Garden

by Tricia Gardella

Illustrated by
Karen Donnelly

For Isaac and Jessica for helping me to grow. —T.G.

To my own Little Helpers who are now pretty much grown. —Karen

This is the salad overflowing its bowl
That comes from Grandpa's garden.

oregano

This is the lettuce, crisp and green,

The tastiest lettuce ever seen.

It forms the bed of a luscious salad
That comes from Grandpa's garden.

This is the radish, red and round,

A special treat
that comes from the ground

And adds some snap to the luscious salad
That comes from Grandpa's garden.

This is the carrot,
orange and thin,

Whose lacy tops dance in the wind.

It's a bright confetti grated into the salad
That comes from Grandpa's garden.

These are the onions,
both stout and spare,
That add a flavor beyond compare

When sliced or chopped
into the luscious salad

That comes from Grandpa's garden.

"snap
"crunch

This is the celery, pale and straight,
Whose essence and texture help to create

A tasty tidbit in the luscious salad
That comes from Grandpa's garden.

These are the beets, pickled or plain,
Painting the lettuce with their rich,
red stain,

And bringing some softness to the
luscious salad
That comes from Grandpa's garden.

This is the cucumber, long and fine,

That's dark and firm when
plucked from the vine

And adds more texture to the luscious salad
That comes from Grandpa's garden.

This is the tomato,
juicy and sweet.

Slices or wedges make a dish complete,

Especially when used to top the salad
That comes from Grandpa's garden.

These are the herbs with a
pungence to savor
Which spread their aroma
and all sorts of flavor

Vinegar

When oiled and vinegared
and tossed with the salad
That comes from Grandpa's garden.

This is the family
ready to eat
A fresh and special
kind of treat.

A treat made of vegetables
gathered into a salad
That comes from
Grandpa's garden.

The End

About the Author

Tricia Gardella's books are mostly influenced by the ranch life she stepped into sixty years ago. She writes children's books about ranch animals, ranch routines, and ranch relationships, though she occasionally gets side-tracked to explore the myriad other sides of life. She has tried it all, and almost mastered some: canning, cooking, knitting and other fiber arts, rug-making, gardening, and various business ventures. But writing is her happiest of places and she is thrilled to be back after a twenty-year sabbatical. She has a BA in Ancient History and Classical Archaeology, three children, seven grandchildren, and three great grandchildren, all giving her much food for thought. She lives with two self-centered cats in Central California.

About the Illustrator

Karen Donnelly has been illustrating books and other things for many many years after a childhood spent drawing for fun, so she couldn't be happier. She lives near the sea with her family and dog who provide constant inspiration and interruptions.

More great books from Tricia Gardella

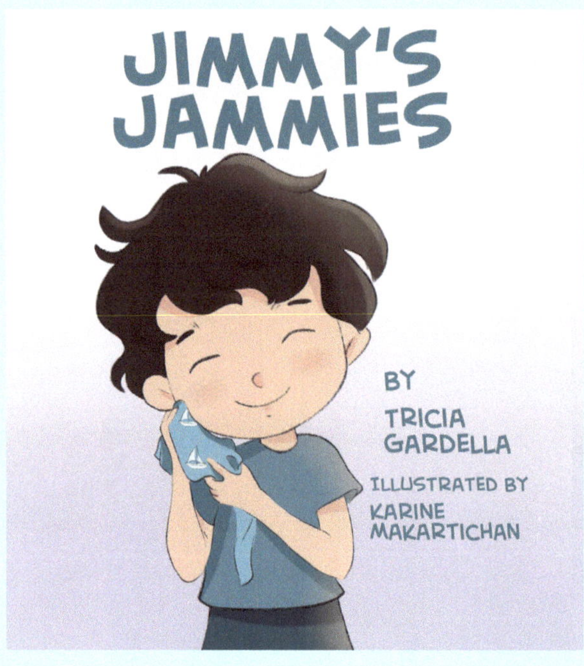

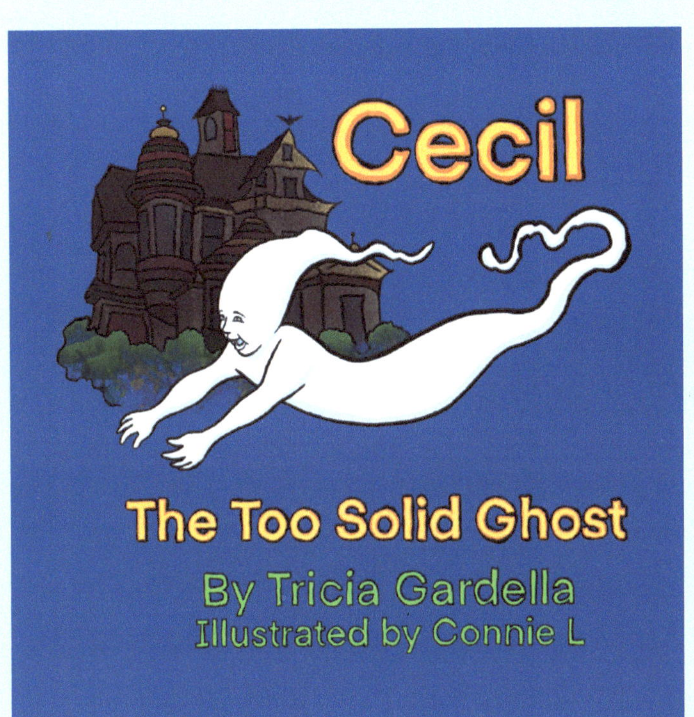

Cecil
The Too Solid Ghost
By Tricia Gardella
Illustrated by Connie L

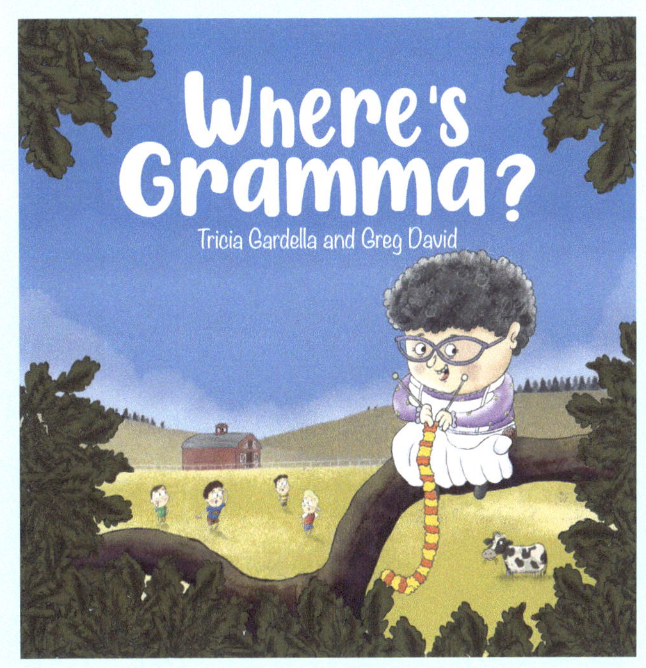

Where's Gramma?
Tricia Gardella and Greg David

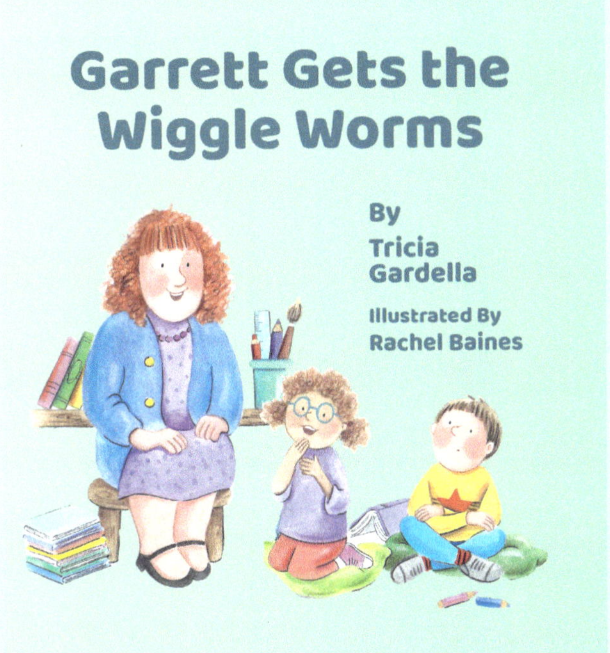

Garrett Gets the Wiggle Worms
By
Tricia Gardella
Illustrated By
Rachel Baines

Just Like My Dad
Tricia Gardella
illustrated by
Margot Apple

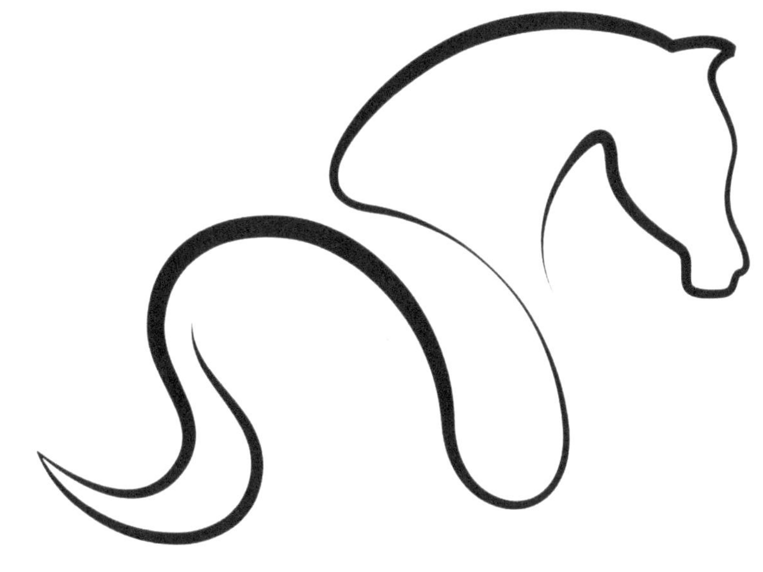

WRITE 'EM COWGIRL PUBLISHING

triciagardella.com